SHORT WALKS
SCOTTISH BORDERS

by Ronald Turnbull

St Cuthbert's Way runs down northeast from Wideopen Hill (Walk 7)

CONTENTS

Using this guide 4
Route summary table 6
Map key 7
Introduction 9
   The story of the Borders 9
   Hill ranges and the River Tweed 10
   Bases and places to stay 11
   Travel 11

The walks
1.	Cove and Cockburnspath	13
2.	St Abb's Head	19
3.	Eyemouth shores	23
4.	Edin's Hall Broch	29
5.	Paxton House and the Tweed	33
6.	Kelso and Roxburgh	39
7.	Wideopen Hill	45
8.	Waterloo Monument	49
9.	St Boswells	55
10.	Eildon Hills	61
11.	Abbotsford and Cauldshiels Loch	67
12.	Hawick and Vertish Hill	73
13.	Bowhill House	79
14.	Peebles and Neidpath Castle	85
15.	Cademuir Hill	91

Useful information 95

USING THIS GUIDE

Routes in this book

In this book you will find a selection of easy or moderate walks suitable for almost everyone, including casual walkers and families with children, or for when you only have a short time to fill. The routes have been carefully chosen to allow you to explore the area and its attractions. Most routes are circular or out-and-back, although some linear walks may be included that use public transport to get back to the start. Although there may be some climbs there is no challenging terrain, but do bear in mind that conditions can sometimes be wet or muddy underfoot. A route summary table is included on page 6 to help you choose the right walk.

Clothing and footwear

You won't need any special equipment to enjoy these walks. The weather in Britain can be changeable, so choose clothing suitable for the season and wear or carry a waterproof jacket. For footwear, comfortable walking boots or trainers with a good grip are best. A small rucksack for drinks, snacks and spare clothing is useful. See www.adventuresmart.uk.

Walk descriptions

At the beginning of each walk you'll find all the information you need:

- start/finish location, with a what3words address to help you find it
- parking and transport information, estimated walking time, total distance and climb
- details of public toilets available along the route and where you can get refreshments
- a summary of the key highlights of the walk and what you might see

Timings given are the time to complete the walk at a reasonable walking pace. Allow extra time for extended stops or if walking with children.

The route is described in clear, easy-to-follow directions, with each waypoint marked on an accompanying map extract. It's a good idea to read the whole of the route instructions before setting out, so that you know what to expect.

Maps, GPX files and what3words

Extracts from the OS® 1:25,000 map accompany each route. GPX files for all the walks in this book are available to download at www.cicerone.co.uk/1251/gpx.

What3words is a free smartphone app which identifies every 3m square of the globe with a unique three-word address, e.g. ///destiny.cafe.sonic. For more information see https://what3words.com/products/what3words-app.

USING THIS GUIDE

Walking with children

Even young children can be surprisingly strong walkers, but every family is different and you may need to adapt the timings given in this book to take that into account. Make sure you go at the pace of the slowest member and choose a walk with an exciting objective in mind, such as a cave, river, waterfall or picnic spot. Many of the walks can be shortened to suit – suggestions are included at the end of the route description.

Dogs

Sheep or cattle may be found grazing on a number of these walks. Keep dogs under control at all times so that they don't scare or disturb livestock or wildlife. Cattle, particularly cows with calves, may occasionally pose a risk to walkers with dogs. If you ever feel threatened by cattle, let go of your dog's lead and let it run free. Always bag and bin dog poo, or take it home.

Enjoying the countryside responsibly

Enjoy the countryside and treat it with respect to protect our natural environments. In Scotland, you can enjoy the outdoors on most land and inland water, as long as you act responsibly and follow the Scottish Outdoor Access Code – www.outdooraccess-scotland.scot.

The Scottish Outdoor Access Code

Responsible access can be enjoyed over most of Scotland including parks, hills, moors, mountains and woods, beaches and the coast, lochs, rivers and canals, and some areas of farmland. The key principles are:

Take responsibility for your own actions
- park sensibly and do not create an obstruction
- take your rubbish home

Respect the interests of other people
- respect the needs of other people enjoying or working in the outdoors
- follow any reasonable advice from land managers
- on farmland, leave gates as you find them and keep to unsown ground, field edges or paths
- access rights do not usually apply to farmyards, but if a well-used path goes through a farmyard, you can follow it
- paths are shared with others – let people know you are coming so you do not alarm them, and slow down, stop or stand aside if needed

Care for the environment
- don't disturb or damage wildlife or historic places
- never light open fires, barbecues or fire bowls in dry periods or near to forests, farmland, buildings or historic sites at any time
- never cut down or damage trees

ROUTE SUMMARY TABLE

WALK NAME	START POINT	TIME	DISTANCE
1. Cove and Cockburnspath	Cove Harbour	4hr	10.5km (6.5 miles)
2. St Abb's Head	Northfield Visitor Centre, St Abbs	2½hr	5.8km (3.6 miles)
3. Eyemouth Shores	Eyemouth seafront	3hr	8.3km (5.2 miles)
4. Edin's Hall Broch	Abbey St Bathans	3¼hr	8.2km (5.1 miles)
5. Paxton House and the Tweed	Paxton House near Berwick-on-Tweed	2¼hr	5.7km (3.5 miles)
6. Kelso and Roxburgh	Tweed Bridge, Kelso	4hr	11.4km (7.1 miles)
7. Wideopen Hill	Cliftoncote Farm, Bowmont Water	3¼hr	7.7km (4.8 miles)
8. Waterloo Monument	Harestanes Centre near Ancrum	3hr	7.3km (4.5 miles)
9. St Boswells	St Boswells main street	2¾hr	7.5km (4.7 miles)
10. Eildon Hills	Melrose Abbey	3¾hr	8.3km (5.2 miles)
11. Abbotsford and Cauldshiels Loch	Abbotsford House near Melrose	4hr	9.6km (6.0 miles)
12. Hawick and Vertish Hill	Drumlanrig's Tower, Hawick	3¼hr	8.6km (5.3 miles)
13. Bowhill House	Bowhill House near Selkirk	3hr	7.7km (4.8 miles)
14. Peebles and Neidpath Castle	Tweed Bridge, Peebles	2hr	5.9km (3.7 miles)
15. Cademuir Hill	Manor Sware, above Peebles	3¾hr	8.8km (5.5 miles)

ROUTE SUMMARY TABLE

HIGHLIGHTS
Coast, nature reserve, castle
Coastal nature reserve, birds, geology
Clifftops, town, harbour
River, broch remains, optional hill
River, gardens, historic bridge
Rivers, castle ruins, viaduct
Grassy uplands with wide views all round
Small hill, monument, gardens
River, abbey ruins (paid-for)
Hills, abbey ruins, river, historic town
Historic house, river, small lochs
Historic town, mills, loch, hill
Lakes, riverside, ruined castle, historic house
River, castle, viaduct, tunnel, historic town
Small hill with Iron Age forts, riverside

SYMBOLS USED ON ROUTE MAPS

 Start point

 Finish point

 Start and finish at the same place

 Waypoint

~ Route line

MAPPING IS SHOWN AT A SCALE OF 1:25,000

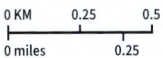

DOWNLOAD THE GPX FILES FOR FREE AT
www.cicerone.co.uk/1251/gpx

The Horse statue, Hawick (Walk 12)

INTRODUCTION

Scott's View of River Tweed with the Eildon Hills (Walk 10)

I wish I could draw you over the Border in summer or autumn, when we could at least visit some places in that land where every valley has its battle, and every stream its song.

Walter Scott, letter to Samuel Robertson, 1831

Scotland isn't just the Highlands and the Lowlands. South of the two great cities of Glasgow and Edinburgh lie the Southern Uplands, the border country. Quite different from the rugged mountains of the north, here are rolling grassy hills, surrounding the wide valley of the River Tweed.

The walking in this area is comparatively gentle – much gentler than the Scottish Highlands, say. Paths are generally good, and those alongside the great rivers give walking that's virtually flat. The hills visited – mostly within that wide Tweed valley – offer wide views and upland atmosphere while remaining modest in height. All of the walks are circular, returning back to where they started.

The story of the Borders

Briefly, the story of the border country can be divided into three chapters. The 'battle valleys' celebrated by Walter Scott look back to the grim times when this was a buffer zone between the two kingdoms of Scotland and England. And buffers receive a battering: not just from the two nations' armies, but from raiding horsemen crossing the hills from any neighbouring valley. Defensive towers and castles rose above Cockburnspath (Walk 1), on the

Eyemouth coast (Walk 3), above the Tweed at Roxburgh (Walk 6), Newark Tower at Bowhill (Walk 13), and Neidpath at Biggar (Walk 14); while one particular campaign by the armies of Henry VIII in 1544 ruined the prosperous abbeys at Kelso (Walk 6), Dryburgh (Walk 9), and Melrose (Walk 10).

The abbeys fell, but the border towns with their sturdy inhabitants survived. And from the 18th century, with the cattle-thief's hills tamed into sheep pastures, the woollen mills alongside the River Tweed brought prosperity. So in Kelso (Walk 6), Hawick (Walk 12), and Peebles (Walk 14) we can start our walks with a tour of the handsome Victorian towns, built from local sandstone.

Prosperity came also to the little fishing ports alongside the North Sea. The first three walks feature rugged clifftops, but also the charming Cove Harbour (Walk 1) and Eyemouth (Walk 2).

The third chapter in this brief history is today. The Borders Region at first adopted the slogan of 'Scotland's Top Short Break Destination'. With its comfortable small towns, those viewpoint hills rising above the countryside, the woods and riversides – not to mention grand and gardened houses like Bowhill (Walk 13), Abbotsford (Walk 11), and Paxton (Walk 5) – it's country that well lives up to its more recent replacement slogan 'Bordering on the brilliant'.

Hill ranges and the River Tweed

The Borders are a vast area, stretching from the North Sea almost across

On Cademuir Hill (Walk 15)

TRAVEL

to the Solway Firth and featuring the hill ranges of the Southern Uplands, the Lammermuirs to the north, and the Cheviots along the English border. This book includes walks within the wide valley of the River Tweed: one of Scotland's great rivers, born high in the hills, this is already wide-flowing and full of salmon as far upstream as Peebles, eventually to become part of the English border as it runs out to Berwick and the sea. Almost as important is its main tributary the Teviot. The recently proposed Borders National Park would have been, basically, the Teviot and its catchment running up into the Cheviots. Seven of the walks in this book feature the banks of these two rivers.

The surrounding hill ranges tend to be big, bleak, and somewhat boggy on top. Instead, we explore some of the smaller ones emerging from the river valley itself. Eildon (Walk 10) and the Waterloo Monument (Walk 8) are the rocky plugs of former volcanoes, while Cademuir above Peebles (Walk 14) and Cauldshiels above Abbotsford (Walk 11) are former Iron Age forts, sited for their wide-ranging views.

Bases and places to stay

Lying within easy reach of Edinburgh, the border country is well supplied with B&Bs and holiday rentals. The historic inns of the countryside are in

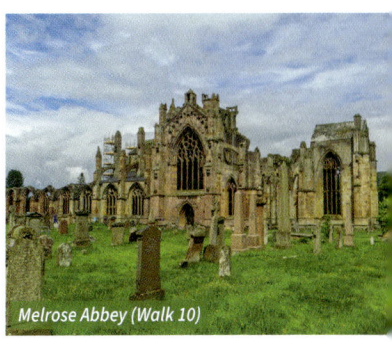
Melrose Abbey (Walk 10)

decline, but you'll find comfortable and charming places to stay in all of the main towns. You can access two or more of the walks in this book from out of Eyemouth, Kelso, the Yetholms, Melrose, Selkirk, Hawick, and Peebles.

Travel

Given the surrounding hills, the Borders aren't well served by railways. The East Coast Main Line runs through Berwick-upon-Tweed; note that while the old county of Berwickshire is Scottish, Berwick itself has, since the 1480s, been captured into England. The other railway, the recently re-opened northern end of the Waverley Line, links Edinburgh with Galashiels and Tweedbank near Melrose. Good bus services link all the main towns to Edinburgh or Berwick. Where not starting in the towns themselves, most of the walks are accessible by bus or, in one case, train.

Cove Harbour

WALK 1
Cove and Cockburnspath

Start/finish	Cove hamlet above Cove Harbour
Locate	///violin.makeovers.grit
Cafes/pubs	Pease Bay holiday park, community shop at Cockburnspath
Transport	Buses from Berwick/Dunbar to Cockburnspath
Parking	Public car park at Cove (TD13 5XD)
Toilets	At Pease Bay holiday park and Cockburnspath

Time 4hr
Distance 10.5km (6.5 miles)
Climb 170m

A longish walk of coast, woodland, and some wonderful bridges

The walk uses the waymarked Southern Upland Way (SU Way) along clifftops and up the wooded Pease Dean. Road walking and farmland lead by the ruined Cockburnspath Tower to historic Cockburnspath. Here you can make a short return by the SU Way, but the full route leads over two bridges and under three more at the second deeply wooded stream, Dunglass Dean.

Garlic wood near Cockburnspath Tower

Above Cove Harbour

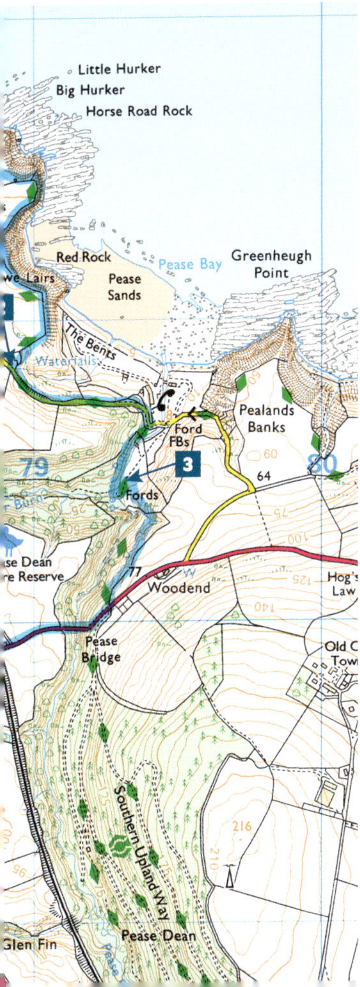

1 A tarred track through a gate would slant down to **Cove Harbour** – explore that at the end of your walk. For now, with the cove down on your left take the track past houses. The signed Coastal Path starts in a tunnel through willow scrub, to open clifftops and a junction with a signpost. Here the SU Way arrives from the right. Follow the clifftop path for nearly 2km to a road above **Pease Sands**.

2 Turn left along the road towards Pease Bay holiday park. Just before a ford and footbridge, take the enclosed path on the right, signposted as SU Way. It leads into the woodland nature reserve with a stream on your left. After 300m turn left over a footbridge. Keep left to cross another footbridge and keep left, downstream, for just 50m, to an SU Way waymark.

3 Take the path sharp right, which rises through woods above the stream, with steps. It runs along the top of the wood to reach the **A1107** road. Turn right across the high bridge over Pease Dean. As the road bends left, keep ahead on an overgrown path. This

Cockburnspath Tower

becomes a track through a wood of wild garlic to **Cockburnspath Tower**. The tower possibly dates back to the 14th century.

4 Before the tower turn up left along a field edge to a stile. Don't cross but move right to a gate and track passing under the A1 to meet a wide but quiet road (the former A1). Turn left along this for 300m to where a track turns back sharp left. Take this to where it bends right; here a signpost indicates a hedged, green track (**Chesterfield Road**) on the right. This track can be overgrown in summer; alternatives are field edges to its left then to its right, or staying on the road (former A1) into Cockburnspath. Follow the hedged green track to a lane.

5 Turn right, down to rejoin the old A1 into **Cockburnspath**. Just before the bus stops on both sides of the road, turn sharp left past the bowling club, then right on a tarmac path to the village centre. The **Cross** marks the start (or end) of the SU Way.

6 Cross into a narrow lane to pass the school (left) and community shop (right). The lane becomes a fenced path signposted as John Muir Way. After a gate go straight across an open field to another gate into woods. Just inside the woods you'll meet a narrow track.

7 Turn down right and at the wood's bottom edge emerge past a lodge to a lane. Turn left over **Dunglass Burn**.

The parapet's quite low and the drop to the stream below about twice as high as you were expecting! At once turn right down a lane to pass under the high stone railway bridge. As the lane ends, take the path signposted 'John Muir Way' through woods, passing under two road bridges.

WALK 1 – COVE AND COCKBURNSPATH

There are five bridges on this walk. You cross over the Dunglass New Bridge (the second oldest!) and the Old Bridge, and go under a concrete A1 bridge and its current replacement built on steel girders, as well as the stone one of the East Coast Main Line.

8 Emerging at a lane end, turn right over Dunglass Old Bridge for a hedged path to a lane. Keep ahead to a roundabout on the **A1**. Take the first exit (Cove and Pease Bay), then the side road signposted to Cove.

Bridges over Dunglass Dean

> **– To shorten**
>
> At the Cross in Cockburnspath, turn right to the main road and then left. Look out for an SU Way marker high on a lamppost to take a track on the right; then follow SU Way markers to the coast near Cove. This shortens the walk to 9km (about 3hr 15min).

Deep Deans

Where streams come down off the Southern Uplands into the soft sandstones of the coast, they carve out deep, steep little valleys named as Deans: formidable obstacles to any army invading from England into Scotland, or vice versa. Cockburnspath Tower passed on this walk is ideally placed to defend any attempted crossing of these: this gave it huge strategic value dominating the coastal lowlands. It was held by the Red Douglases against their local warlord rivals the Home (pronounced Hume) family.

St Abbs Harbour from White Heugh

WALK 2
St Abb's Head

Start/finish	*Northfield Visitor Centre, just outside St Abbs*
Locate	*///fruity.pods.revisits*
Cafes/pubs	*Cafes at start and at St Abbs Harbour*
Transport	*Bus from Berwick to St Abbs stops near Northfield visitor centre*
Parking	*At visitor centre (TD14 5QF), or pay-and-display in St Abbs*
Toilets	*At start and St Abbs Harbour*

Time 2½hr
Distance 5.8km (3.6 miles)
Climb 170m

A clifftop nature reserve famous for its birds and baby seals

St Abb's Head is visited by 60,000 nesting seabirds every year and roughly the same number of human beings – in high summer this is a busy walk. Meanwhile, seals are breeding in the stony coves below between October and December. Make time to pop down to St Abbs itself, with its pretty harbour. Its small visitor centre (separate from the National Trust for Scotland (NTS) one at the walk start) has telescopes for viewing the birds.

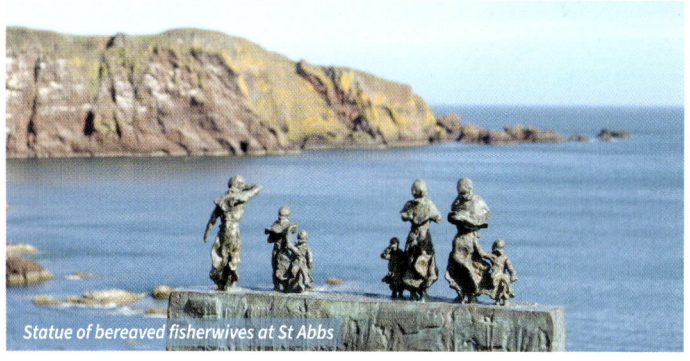
Statue of bereaved fisherwives at St Abbs

1 With the NTS visitor centre on your left, cross a farmyard to a field-edge path beside the road. After 300m turn left on the wide path signposted for St Abb's Head. Or to visit St Abbs village and harbour cross the road for a wide path to its right. The path runs for 250m beside a high wall to a picnic table high above **Starney Bay**.

Guillemots on sea stacks at St Abb's Head

2 The clear path continues above cliffs and White Heugh peninsular, with its chimneystacks rock formation. Drop with a fence to your left to a first bay, **Burnmouth Harbour**. The path runs to left (inland) of a grassy knoll to the next one, **Horsecastle Bay**. Then it passes along the inland side of **Kirk Hill** to a junction with signpost.

3 For the main route, keep ahead, with a fence to the right and purple arrows. The path slants up to clifftops, with the lighthouse ahead.

From the clifftops of St Abb's Head Nature Reserve, between April and July, you can see and hear – and, indeed, smell – the nesting seabirds whose guano or dung leaves white streaks down the cliffs. Look out for guillemots, razorbills, and kittiwakes; there could just possibly be a puffin.

St Abbs Harbour

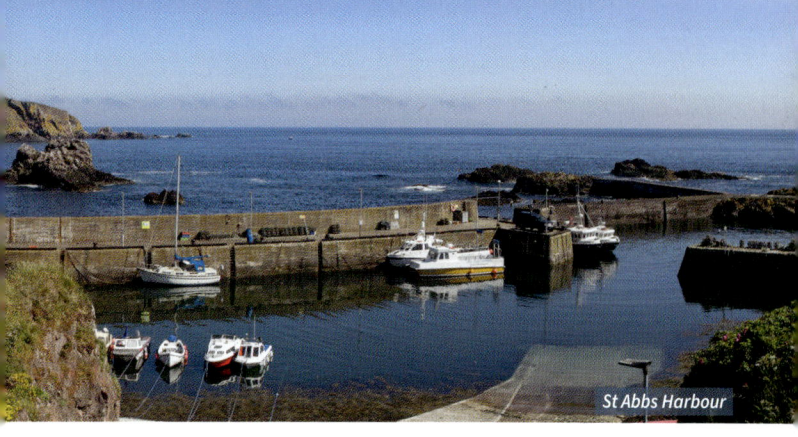

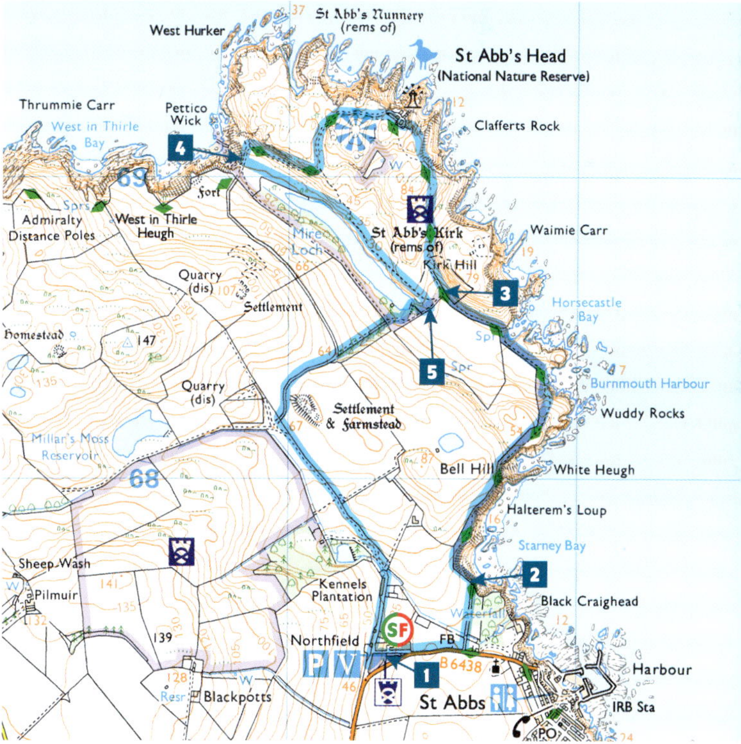
St Abb's Nunnery
(rems of)
West Hurker
St Abb's Head
(National Nature Reserve)
Thrummie Carr
Pettico Wick
West in Thirle Bay
Clafferts Rock
4
Fort
Admiralty Distance Poles
West in Thirle Heugh
St Abb's Kirk
(rems of)
Kirk Hill
Waimie Carr
Mire Loch
Quarry (dis)
Settlement
3
Horsecastle Bay
Homestead
147
5
Burnmouth Harbour
Quarry (dis)
Settlement & Farmstead
Wuddy Rocks
Millar's Moss Reservoir
68
Bell Hill
White Heugh
Halterem's Loup
Starney Bay
2
Sheep Wash
Pilmuir
Kennels Plantation
Black Craighead
Waterfall
SF
139
Northfield
FB
B6438
Harbour
1
Resr
Blackpotts
St Abbs
IRB Sta
PO

Sea mist above Mire Loch

Pass above the lighthouse keeper's house to a small car park and follow its tarmac access track down towards the natural harbour at **Pettico Wick**. A path leads down towards the little bay, though its bottom end has been carried away by a small landslip.

4 Directly above the bay, turn left at a waymark post to head inland on a grass path. Bear left and pass to the left of a reed bed and then left of the **Mire Loch**. Above the foot of the loch you'll see the path you used on the outward walk and the shortcut path running across below you. Bear right to join this path directly below, turning right towards the foot of Mire Loch.

5 At once turn right again on a smaller path which runs along the loch's dam to emerge at the end of a gravel track. Follow this ahead to a gate and a corner of the tarred access track. Follow this ahead, descending through fields then past houses to **Northfield** visitor centre.

> **− To shorten**
>
> At Waypoint 3 turn left to rejoin the main route at the foot of Mire Loch, giving a walk of 3.5km with 80m climb (1hr 30min).
>
> **+ To lengthen**
>
> From the lighthouse cottages, you can continue on faint paths along the clifftops, including the isolated promontory of the former St Abb's Nunnery. Above Pettico Wick, keep left along the top of steep slopes to join the tarmac track at the bend where it turns downhill towards the sea. This will extend the walk to 6.5km with 230m climb (about 2hr 45min).

WALK 3
Eyemouth shores

Start/finish	*Fishermen's memorial, Eyemouth seafront*
Locate	*///rise.suspended.cello*
Cafes/pubs	*Cafes and fish and chips at Eyemouth Harbour*
Transport	*Frequent buses from Edinburgh, Dunbar, and Berwick*
Parking	*On seafront next to the Co-op (TD14 5EU)*
Toilets	*At top end of harbour*

Time 3hr
Distance 8.3km (5.2 miles)
Climb 100m

A beach, an ancient but busy harbour, and clifftop walking above two different sorts of rock

Since Berwick got absorbed into England in 1482, Eyemouth has been the main harbour of southeastern Scotland. It is still busy with fishing boats, yachts, and servicing the offshore wind industry. As well as the charming harbour, the walk takes in fine shorelines which in the east are tough, layered grey sandstone from the ocean floor and in the west are jumbly red-brown volcanic lava. There's also a surprise woodland moment alongside the River Eye.

Coastal path east of Eyemouth

SHORT WALKS SCOTTISH BORDERS

1 With the beach down to your left, follow the sea wall round into the harbour. At its top end turn left onto a pier running back towards the sea. Towards the end of the pier a bridge leads onto the shore again. Turn left along the harbour, passing below historic Gunsgreen House, then take steps up right and turn left on a tarmac path.

2 Keep ahead to drop across a car park. Head up the grass bank opposite to a sudden view of the sea. Turn right on a small path along low clifftops, round to a gate alongside the golf course. Through the gate turn left onto a smaller path left of a wall. Follow this for just 50m, past the head of **Ramfauds** inlet, to a waymark post in front of the notorious 6th green of Eyemouth Golf Club.

> ⓘ *Gunsgreen House above Eyemouth harbour was built by John Adam in 1753 for prosperous smuggler John Nesbit.*

> **The back tee of the 6th hole requires a long drive right across the sea inlet to the green in front of you. Having lost one ball into the inlet, you may move onto the forward tee for an easier shot.**

3 In front of the green turn off left, on a much smaller path, around the edge of the golf course. The small, waymarked path continues above the rocky foreshore. After 400m ignore a

Eyemouth Harbour in sea mist

WALK 3 – EYEMOUTH SHORES

signposted path inland across the golf course. After another 800m, at the point called **Daring**, a three-way signpost marks the path to take inland.

4 The clear path soon has a rose hedge to your right. Cross a road to continue to the left of the 17th hole of the golf course to a tarmac lane. Cross right and left to a tarmac path downhill. This passes to right of a **school** and across a residential street to reach the A1107 road.

5 Cross and turn right, to cross the River Eye. Now turn unexpectedly left to find a signpost on the left marked 'River Eye Footpath'. Head down earth

River Eye reaches Eyemouth Harbour

WALK 3 – EYEMOUTH SHORES

Above Killiedraught Bay

steps to pass back under the A1107. The riverside path is rugged, then wide, and emerges at a road with a church and steeple opposite.

6 Cross the road on your right and continue along Albert Road to its end. Turn left up the main road towards Coldingham. At the top of the hill, turn right into Pocklaw Slap. Where the street bends left, keep ahead on a track to the corner of **Killiedraught Bay** and a fingerpost.

7 Turn back sharp right to pass along the clifftops and below the **holiday park**. Where the path arrives at a sudden view down to Eyemouth Sands, a signpost indicates the path left to the **Eyemouth Fort**. Make a loop around the end of the promontory and return by the same path to the signpost.

8 Continue above the cliffs to a path junction, where you fork down left onto the shingle beach. If there's a very high tide stay on the higher path. Follow the beach round until a concrete ramp leads up to the beginning of the sea wall. Follow it above the beach to return to the walk start.

− To shorten

At Waypoint 6 just turn right to rejoin the outward route at Eyemouth Harbour, reducing the distance to 6km (2hr).

Eyemouth seen from above the harbour

Eyemouth Fort

On the interpretation board Eyemouth Fort appears as an early version of the nearby holiday village… It was built in 1547 by an occupying English army, demolished in 1550 as part of a peace treaty, rebuilt by Scotland's French allies in 1557, and demolished again following the 1559 Treaty of Cateau-Cambresis. Eyemouth Museum has a Virtual Reality version of it during its second brief period of existence.

Cannon at Eyemouth Fort

WALK 4
Edin's Hall Broch

Start/finish	Cafe by riverside at southwest end of Abbey St Bathans
Locate	///treatable.distract.canyons
Cafes/pubs	Cafe at start (often closed at weekends)
Transport	No public transport
Parking	At start (TD11 3TX), or near A6112 at track top of Elba Cottage
Toilets	No public toilets on route

Time 3¼hr
Distance 8.2km (5.1 miles)
Climb 150m

A long and fairly rugged walk of footbridges and woodlands, to an ancient broch above Whiteadder Water

The hidden village of Abbey St Bathans takes its name from an Irish monk. But the more notable visitor was the gruesome three-headed giant Red Edin, founder of Edinburgh itself (perhaps). He is said to have built a large, thick-walled stone tower high above the river; its impressive walls remain to a height of about 2m. The path to reach it involves woodlands and field edges, plus two footbridges high above Whiteadder Water.

Path sign and autumn rowan at Abbey St Bathans

SHORT WALKS SCOTTISH BORDERS

1 There's a ford through the river, but it's better to head upstream behind the SU Way shelter to cross a high footbridge. Go straight over the track from the ford onto a wooded path signed for Elba Footbridge. The path soon runs across scrubby grassland above the river to reach a track. Turn left, signed for Elba Bridge, up through **Butterwell Wood** to its top.

2 Turn sharp right into a side track along the top of the wood. This descends to meet a tarmac lane. Turn down right for 250m. Just above **Retreat House** (a small mansion), bend left over a stone bridge to pass above the house and into woods. Keep ahead on the main track, with the river occasionally seen down on your right. After almost 2km it runs into a wider track.

Crossing the Elba footbridge

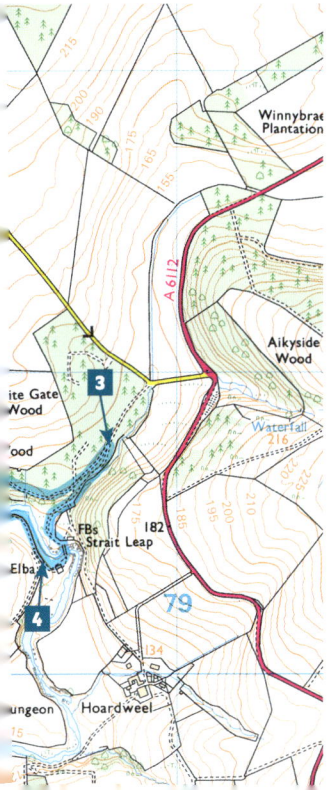

3 Turn down sharp right to the Whiteadder Water, locally pronounced as 'Wittada'. Before a ford, turn left to find the footbridge hidden in foliage. It crosses a rocky corner of the river towards **Elba** cottage. Turn right in front of the cottage's garden; the path crosses a track and runs up through woods to a field alongside the river.

4 Follow the right edge of the field for 600m. Where a wall crosses ahead, go through its gateway and turn up to the right of the wall across the flat field. A path slants to the right up a steeper banking. Continue along the top of this banking, then above a wall to a wall stile. Continue above a fence to a kissing gate onto open hill. A rather steep path slants up the hill slope ahead to its crest. Turn up through earth ramparts to the remains of **Edin's Hall**.

Beside Whiteadder river with Cockburn Law ahead

The fortified stone tower lies within the lumpy remains of an Iron Age settlement, all on top of an older hill fort. The broch had walls 4m thick, with passages and stairways inside them.

5 Immediately above the broch, a fence across the hillside has a field gate, with a stile to its left. Cross the stile and turn right beside the fence then on a path across a downhill corner of the field, to reach a stile and signpost. Here you could turn uphill for Cockburn Law. The clear path ahead, signposted 'Abbey St Bathans', slants down towards the river to the flatter ground of the valley floor. It briefly runs next to a fence, but keep ahead when the fence turns away to right.

6 At a birch-shaded stream the path turns left to a footbridge, then up steps to a corner of the tarmac road. Named Toot Corner, it has a sign inviting motorists to sound their horn on approaching. Keep ahead, down into **Abbey St Bathans**. As you join the river, a path bears right over a small footbridge to run beside the main river back to the walk start.

+ To lengthen

From the signpost after Edin's Hall, head uphill on very sketchy paths to the hill fort viewpoint of Cockburn Law, giving a walk of 10.5km with 250m climb (4hr).

Edin's Hall Broch

WALK 5
Paxton House and the Tweed

Time 2¼hr
Distance 5.7km (3.5 miles)
Climb 100m

Good paths take in the mighty River Tweed and a feat of 19th-century engineering

Start/finish	Paxton House, west of Berwick-upon-Tweed
Locate	///alert.scrolled.drumbeat
Cafes/pubs	Tea room at Paxton House
Transport	Bus 42 Berwick–Duns to walk start
Parking	Car park at start (TD15 1SZ)
Toilets	At Paxton House courtyard

At Paxton House woodland and parkland and a small formal garden surround a stately home stuffed with antiques. But there are two real stars of this walk: the River Tweed, tidal at this point and so wide it can even have a feel of the sea about it; and the ground-breaking suspension bridge, the first of its kind, still carrying traffic across to England. There is a charge for Paxton's grounds (open 10am–5pm; booking is advised if you want to tour the house as well).

Tweed riverside below Paxton House

1 Start at the small entrance for the ticket office shop at the eastern side of **Paxton House**. Navigating the first 50m of this walk is tricky – much easier after that! Facing away from the house, bear right across the end of the car park and across grass, passing the left end of an avenue of little birch trees. Behind two bush-like trees you'll find the top of a gravel path descending to the right under trees. It passes above the adventure playground to a boathouse beside the River Tweed.

2 Turn left, upstream, on a clear path under trees. After 400m the path crosses a footbridge and bends inland above the stream in its eroded, wooded mini-ravine, **Linn Dean**.

The Edinburgh Window at Paxton House

Statue of Capt. Samuel Brown by Union Bridge, Paxton

Follow the path through woods and clearings to the entrance driveway. Cross to a gravel track opposite to pass the Edinburgh Window.

> The Edinburgh Window was recovered from an 1850s insurance office in Princes Street and hidden away for 25 years at Edinburgh Art School, before being re-erected here.

3 The track diminishes to a wide path, until you see a handsome lodge house with pine-log porch on your right. Here the path bends left over a little bridge, but instead keep ahead to join the lodge's driveway. After it bends

WALK 5 – PAXTON HOUSE AND THE TWEED

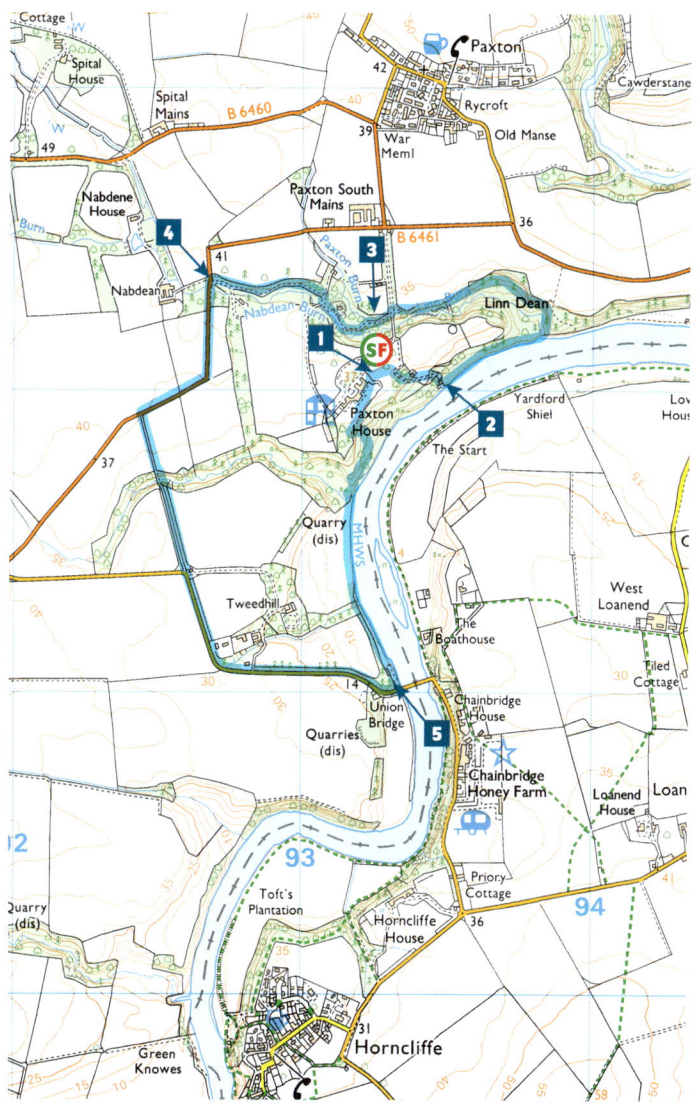

35

Union Bridge, Paxton

to the right, follow the main track left (rather than a side track ahead). After 400m you arrive at the **B6461** road.

4 Turn left along the road for 400m to a right bend, and then continue along it for another 300m to a green-hedged track on the left, signposted to the Union Bridge. After 300m this descends steps to a footbridge, then rises again and runs to a corner of a minor road. Keep ahead along the road to the historic **Union Bridge**. You can walk out onto the bridge to visit England.

5 At the start of the bridge, a good path descends left to the riverbank and follows the Scottish side downstream. After an extended duckboard section, it passes through a doorway in a wall and crosses a footbridge. At once fork left up a path which zigzags away from the river, through ornamental woodland, to emerge suddenly in front of **Paxton House**. Pass along the lawns of the formal garden to a hedge gap and the walk start point.

Paxton House and formal garden

− To shorten

At the riverside (Waypoint 2) turn upstream to the Union Bridge (Waypoint 5), then retrace your steps along the main walk. This reduces the walk to 3km with 50m climb (about 1hr 15min).

✚ To lengthen

At the Union Bridge – and provided you don't mind adventuring into England – you can cross and turn upstream. After 600m fork left for an upper path to Horncliffe, returning along the riverbank. This adds 4km and 50m (about 1hr 30min).

The Union Bridge

Wrought-iron chain link on Union Bridge

It was an enterprising sea captain from the Napoleonic Wars, Samuel Brown, who worked out that the exotic new material wrought iron could be used to make a suspension bridge strong enough for heavy traffic. The bridge, opened in 1820, was the first of its kind, and was studied and imitated by Thomas Telford for his Menai Bridge a few years later. After major restoration in 2021–23, about half of the original ironwork is still functional.

Roxburgh Viaduct over River Teviot

WALK 6
Kelso and Roxburgh

Time 4hr
Distance 11.4km (7.1 miles)
Climb 70m

A level ramble along flowery riverbanks to a spectacular high viaduct

Start/finish	Tweed Bridge, Kelso
Locate	///happening.distilled.swordfish
Cafes/pubs	A choice of cafes around Kelso centre (The Square)
Transport	Buses/coaches from Berwick-upon-Tweed and Edinburgh
Parking	Car parks at start of Teviot riverside path (TD5 8LT), or in Kelso town behind the abbey
Toilets	In Kelso centre, at north corner of The Square

The Teviot is the second great river of the Borders and runs into the Tweed just above Kelso's bridge. On its delightful riverside path you will see plenty of wildflowers, and there'll probably be a heron. You also pass under the remains of Roxburgh Castle. At Roxburgh village you rise above the river for a high railway viaduct, after which the former railbed gives a wooded and scenic return route to Kelso.

Junction Pool and Floors Castle

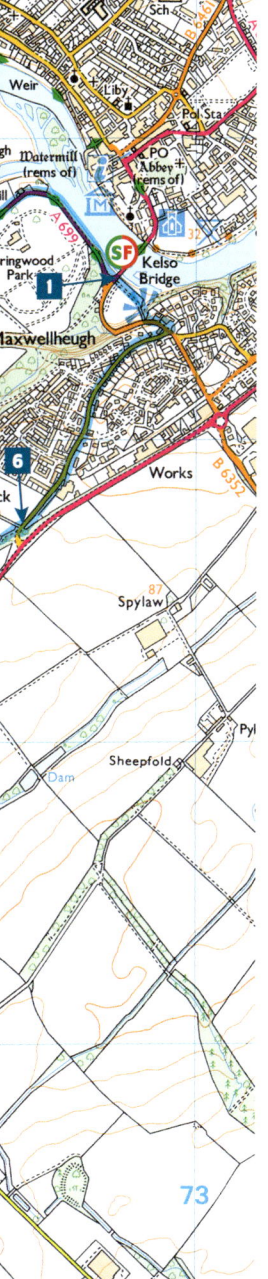

WALK 6 – KELSO AND ROXBURGH

1 From the end of the bridge, follow the pavement of the **A699**. You'll pass Junction Pool and continue alongside the River Teviot to cross **Teviot Bridge**, which has a very narrow pavement. In 50m turn left through a gravel parking area to the riverside path. Car drivers can start and end the route at this point.

2 Follow the delightful path alongside the **River Teviot** for 3.5km. In high summer the riverbank is dominated by white, frothy meadowsweet and blue cranesbill. After 1km you pass below the remnants of **Roxburgh Castle**. After 1.5km and again after 2.5km, small shelter huts are beside the path. The path eventually moves up to field edges above the river and a stile leads onto a lane near Roxburgh.

3 Turn left to pass **Roxburgh Mill** farm. In another 150m, turn left through a gate with a 'Please close the gate' sign. A small path (with an overgrown ditch to right of it) leads to the riverside and onwards upstream. After 400m, with the viaduct rising magnificent ahead, you reach the corner of a track, with a **Borders Abbeys Way** signpost. Turn right, with the fallen remains of Wallace's Tower, a pele tower, seen on the right. Where the track bends right, take steps ahead to a back lane. Follow the lane left, then

River Teviot near Roxburgh Castle

take a gate above into the churchyard. Some ancient gravestones lean against the front of the church.

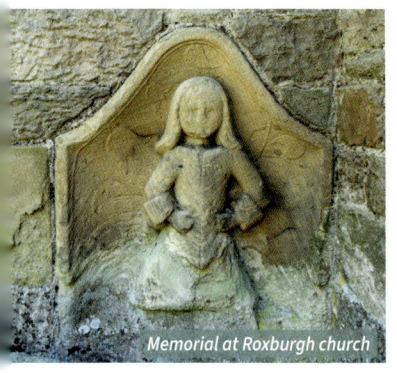
Memorial at Roxburgh church

4 Beyond the church turn left on the main street through **Roxburgh** village. Where the road bends right, keep ahead to a small car park under the piers of a former railway bridge. On the left, the left-hand of the two railway-line paths is signposted for Kelso. Take this to cross the **Roxburgh Viaduct** high above River Teviot.

5 Follow the railbed path for 2.5km, with some distant glimpses left of the spiky-roofed Floors Castle. The well-made path drops right, off the embankment, and rambles up through scrubby woodland to reach a road at the edge of **Kelso**.

6 The noisy A698 is just ahead but keep left, along a wide but quiet street with a pavement. This is the old Jedburgh Road, running down to meet the main B6352 at a petrol station. Cross just up from the mini-roundabout and head downhill to the Millennium Viewpoint over Kelso. Steps down to the right lead into a riverside park. Some more steps lead up onto **Kelso Bridge**. Cross the bridge for the short walk past the abbey ruins (open most days) to The Square with its cafes.

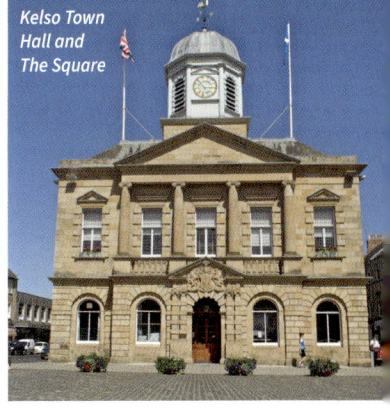

Kelso Town Hall and The Square

The foot of Crookedshaws Hill, heading down towards Yetholm

WALK 7
Wideopen Hill

Start/finish	End of track to Cliftoncote Farm, Bowmont Water
Locate	///noun.relishing.tennis
Cafes/pubs	Pub in Kirk Yetholm
Transport	No public transport
Parking	Limited parking on verge 200m south of the start (TD5 8PU)
Toilets	No public toilets on route

Time 3¼hr
Distance 7.7km (4.8 miles)
Climb 250m

A grassy but quite strenuous ridgeline along the edge of the Cheviots overlooking the wide valley of the Tweed

The grassy ridgeline from Grubbit Law over Wideopen and Crookedshaw Hills is just as nice as its three names. Paths are faint and there are some quite tiring climbs; but it's worth it for the way you look out across the wide plains of the north, or up the narrow Bowmont and Kale valleys into the heart of the Cheviot Hills.

St Cuthbert's Way marker on Crookedshaws Hill

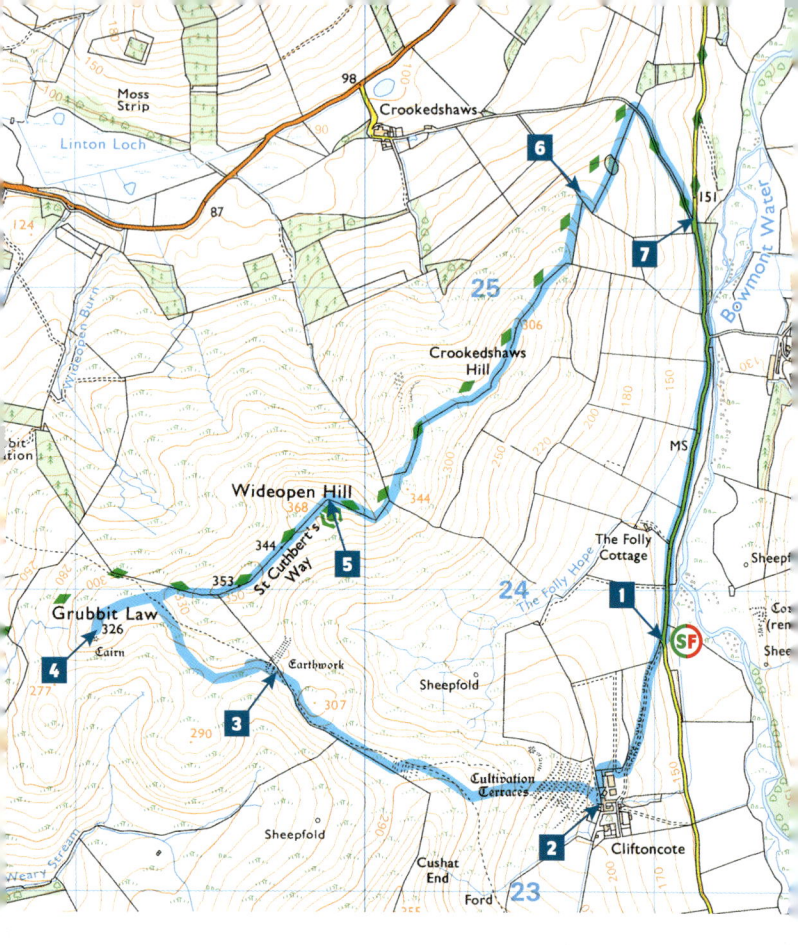

1 Head up the tarmac farm driveway (signposted for Grubbit Law and Morebattle) and fork right across a cattle grid to farm buildings. Take a gate on the right of the buildings and head up the field edge to another gate. Here pass back above the buildings onto open grassy hillside.

2 Above the largest of the sheds, a faint quad bike track heads directly uphill through bracken. As the slope eases, don't continue up the hill slope to left, **Cushat End**. Instead bear right, contouring on a very faint path, to join a ridgeline fence up on your left. The path continues to the right of the

46

WALK 7 – WIDEOPEN HILL

fence, dipping to a col where the fence becomes a wall, then over a slight rise to a small gate in the wall.

3 Through the gate, contour forward on a faint path, which fades as you reach a level little shoulder. Just beyond this a rough track leads up to the right, to the ridgeline east of Grubbit Law. Follow the grass path left, to the nearby summit of **Grubbit Law**, with its small cairn and large view.

4 Return across the col, slanting up left to join a wall. At a crossing wall, take the ladder stile ahead. In 400m the wall bends right at the summit of **Wideopen Hill**. Wideopen Hill is both the high point and the half-way point of St Cuthbert's Way, which runs between Melrose and Lindisfarne.

5 Follow the wall as it bends downhill, turns sharp left, and continues down to a ladder stile. The path rises a little, then continues to right of the

> ⓘ *The 100km long St Cuthbert's Way runs from Melrose to Holy Island in Northumberland tracing the route taken by monks with St Cuthbert's corpse to escape from the Vikings.*

Leaving the summit of Wideopen Hill on St Cuthbert's Way

Looking down Crookedshaws Hill towards Yetholm

wall for 800m along and down **Crookedshaws Hill** to a gate in the wall. Go through this and descend on a path through bracken to a field gate with a walker's gate alongside.

6 Slant right down the open field, to the right-hand edge of a clump of trees, or if the field is under cultivation, turn right along its top and down its right-hand edge. Pass through the trees and on down the field's edge to its bottom right corner. A grassy track leads down to the right, to the lane below.

7 Here St Cuthbert's Way turns sharp left towards Kirk Yetholm, but instead keep ahead along the lane for 1.5km back to the walk start.

– To shorten

From Waypoint 3 continue directly uphill on quad bike tracks to the right of the wall to join the path up Wideopen Hill, reducing the distance to 6.5km with 230m of ascent (about 2hr 45min).

WALK 8
Waterloo Monument

Start/finish	Harestanes Centre, near Ancrum
Locate	///tightrope.crimson.delivers
Cafes/pubs	Cafes at Harestanes (two) and Woodside Walled Garden
Transport	Bus 68 Galashiels–Tweedbank rail station–Jedburgh stops at Cleikemin cottage 1.1km from start
Parking	Car park at Harstanes Centre (TD8 6UQ)
Toilets	At start and Woodside Walled Garden

Time 3hr
Distance 7.3km (4.5 miles)
Climb 200m

Occasionally muddy walking to take in a towering monument, a fairly small hill, and a riverside garden

Peniel Heugh is a small volcanic hump left over from the Carboniferous Period. This waymarked route is on tracks and paths, and the views at the top are extensive – including vertically upwards, at the 50m-high stone tower of the Waterloo Monument which tops the hill. The route continues along the riverside and takes you past the gardens of Monteviot House. Some of the paths get muddy in winter or after heavy rain.

Descending from Waterloo Monument towards Monteviot

Waterloo Monument

1 Head north along the entrance driveway, into a hedged path to its right. Before reaching the **B6400** the path bends right, through a strip of wood with big beeches, and passes a pond to arrive at a junction just before a footbridge.

2 Ignoring this bridge turn left, on a path which soon crosses the B6400, to a signpost. Woodside Walled Garden is on the left here: a garden centre with a fine cafe. The main path keeps right, over the stream. In another 400m the path is about to recross the stream; just before this footbridge, turn off right on a small path through **Divet Ha' Wood**. After 100m meet a gravel track and turn right for 200m, to a rougher track on the left. From here to Waypoint 4 you'll follow green waymark arrows, sometimes faded.

3 Turn up this rougher track, which runs through woods to meet a lane. Cross to the right, to a tall sign forbidding vehicles. Walk around the gate onto a woodland track. After 400m fork left; at once fork left again. At the next fork, you see the Waterloo Monument on the right, but instead fork left for third time, signposted for Peniel Heugh. The wide path leads through woods, then up the wood edge onto the open hilltop of **Peniel Heugh**, with the tall Waterloo Monument ahead.

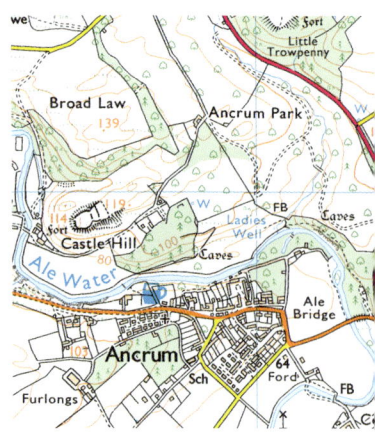

WALK 8 – WATERLOO MONUMENT

Footbridge in Monteviot woods (crossed on the shortened walk)

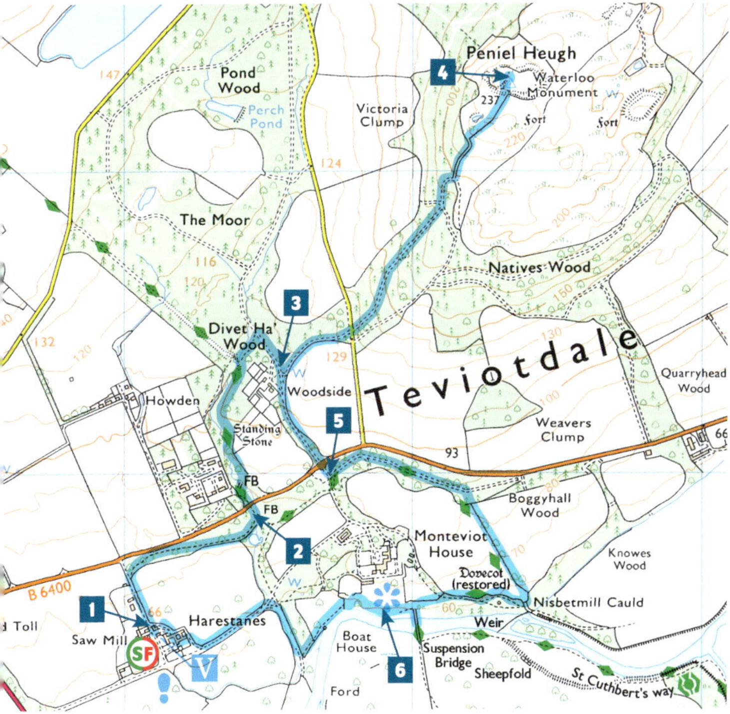

Path to Peniel Haugh and Waterloo Monument

> ⓘ *Peniel Heugh is the basalt plug of one of the volcanoes that existed hereabouts in Carboniferous times. Others in sight include Rubers Law and the Eildons.*

The 45m-high tower was built between 1817 and 1824 to commemorate the Battle of Waterloo.

4 If you've wandered around the tower and are disoriented: from the tower itself pass to right of the trig point to find the top of the rough path you came up on. Continue away from the monument with a fence to your left. Go down the way you came, to cross the first lane and follow the rough track below. Back at Waypoint 3 turn left to join a tarmac driveway to the B6400. Cross into the tarmac driveway of **Monteviot House**.

> Monteviot is an 18th-century lodge built on an ancient site; the Roman Dere Street, used by today's St Cuthbert's Way, runs past the house. The large and varied gardens are open to the public from April to October.

WALK 8 – WATERLOO MONUMENT

5 At once turn left along the path signed as St Cuthbert's Way, through woods then bending right, through fields, to woods beside the **River Teviot**. Turn right on a woodland path with glimpses of the river. A wooden walkway on the left is the start of the high **suspension bridge**: wander out and return before continuing upstream to right of the river.

6 Keep ahead along the foot of Monteviot's garden. After a fisherman's hut turn right, away from the river, on a track under trees. Bear left to a signpost and keep left along a tarred driveway. In 300m turn right, signposted 'Craft Courtyard', to a door through a wall into the Harestanes complex.

> **– To shorten**
>
> To miss out the climb up to Waterloo Monument, at Waypoint 2 cross the footbridge and turn left at the junction just beyond to reach Waypoint 5. This gives a route of 4km with negligible climb (about 1hr 15min).

River Teviot at Monteviot Garden

Dryburgh Abbey

WALK 9
St Boswells

Start/finish	*Top of Hamilton Place, St Boswells*
Locate	*///bossy.care.scrolled*
Cafes/pubs	*Cafe/bookshop in Main Street*
Transport	*Buses from Tweedbank rail station, or direct from Edinburgh/Berwick-upon-Tweed*
Parking	*On-street parking in Main Street (TD6 0AU)*
Toilets	*At entrance to Dryburgh Abbey*

Time 2¾hr
Distance 7.5km (4.7 miles)
Climb 50m

An easy-going walk along both banks of the Tweed, passing Dryburgh Abbey

This walk heads out from St Boswells along the river, to pass the entrance to Dryburgh Abbey. Of all the ruined abbeys of the Borders, Dryburgh is the one Sir Walter Scott chose to be buried in. For those of us still alive, there's now an entrance charge: well worth paying, as the ruins are beautiful (especially in snowdrop time) and aren't seen from the riverside paths on either bank. That riverside walking is on good paths, through fields and woods, with a slightly rocky section on leaving St Boswells. There's also a fine suspension footbridge and a temple to a poet you probably haven't heard of.

Mertoun Bridge

SHORT WALKS SCOTTISH BORDERS

1 Hamilton Place is opposite the corner of an open space on the other side of Main Street. Where Hamilton Place bends left, turn right on a tarmac lane, now following St Cuthbert's Way waymarkers. At once fork left twice, onto a wide earth path. This descends through woodlands above a stream to the **River Tweed**.

2 Turn left over a footbridge and up the Tweed, with steps and bits of boardwalk, to reach a high, green suspension footbridge. Cross this.

Up to the left, a temple of the muses is inspired by the pre-Romantic poet James Thomson, the 'Bard of Elphin'. He's known for his landscape poem *The Seasons*: 'The Black-bird whistles from the thorny Brake; The mellow Bullfinch answers from the Grove.' He died in 1748.

3 Now following **Borders Abbeys Way** waymarkers, keep right along a lane to the entrance of the driveway towards **Dryburgh Abbey**. At the

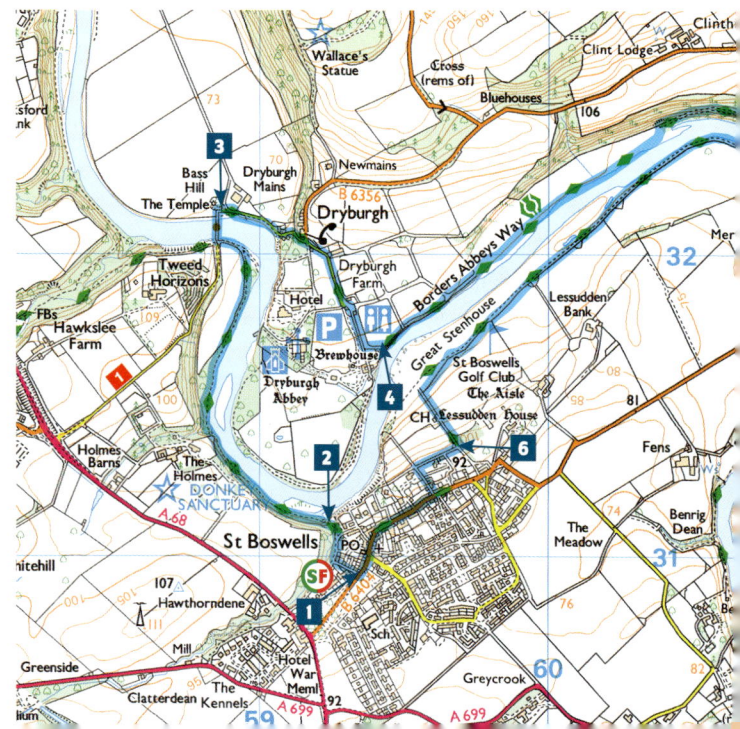

River Tweed above Mertoun Bridge

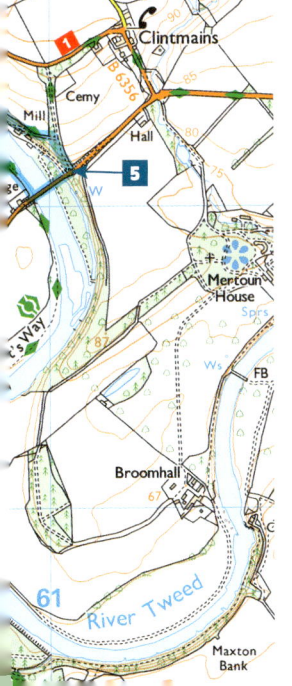

entrance gates of the paid-for abbey grounds, instead bear left past toilets along a lane which becomes a track. A stile and gate on the left start a path beside the abbey grounds to the River Tweed.

4 A wide grass path runs downstream. After 1.5km it becomes a gravel track slanting up into woods above the river. Where the track bends left, keep ahead through a gate for a path along the bottom of a field, above riverbank cliffs of crumbly mudstone. Another gate leads onto an earth track. In a few steps, fork right on a path signposted for Mertoun Bridge. This path leads down to the roadside beside the handsome, sandstone **Mertoun Bridge**.

St Boswell's Main Street

> ⓘ Mertoun Bridge was built in 1837 with stone piers and a wooden superstructure. The wooden bits were carried away in a flood two years later.

5 Cross the bridge (no pavement) and at once turn right, with a signpost for St Cuthbert's Way, down duckboard steps to the riverbank. Follow the river back upstream. The riverside path is overgrown in high summer, but the field edge to its left can be followed instead. After 1km the path runs slightly back from the river, along the left side of the **golf course**. After another 1km take a tarmac track up left towards **St Boswells**, waymarked as St Cuthbert's Way.

6 At the top of a fairly steep ascent, take the lane to the right signed 'Exit right'. It has a high wall to the left and views over the river. In 200m the lane bends left to the top of Main Street. Turn right, down past shops and a cafe/bookshop, to the walk start.

> ⓘ St Boswells is named after St Boisil, a monk of Melrose Abbey. He acted as a teacher to St Cuthbert, and St Cuthbert's Way now runs through the village.

> **− To shorten**
> Walk the best bit of riverside to Dryburgh, tour the abbey, and return the same way for a walk of 5km with 50m climb (about 2hr).

Borders Abbeys

Dryburgh Abbey in daffodil time

Ruined abbeys at Melrose, Jedburgh, Kelso, and here at Dryburgh are linked by the 110km Borders Abbeys Way. All four abbeys were destroyed by the armies of England's Henry VIII as part of the wars called the 'Rough Wooing'. He hoped this campaign would persuade the Scots to marry off the infant Queen Mary to his son Edward. Henry's general, Lord Hertford, was eventually defeated by a scratch force of locals 5km south of here at Ancrum Moor.

The Rhymer's Stone, Eildon Hills

WALK 10
Eildon Hills

Time 3¾hr
Distance 8.3km (5.2 miles)
Climb 350m

Exploring a fine old town, the Tweed, and the hill so seductive the Queen of the Fairies lives inside it

Start/finish	*Melrose Abbey*
Locate	*///troll.skirting.gasping*
Cafes/pubs	*Cafes and pubs in Melrose High Street*
Transport	*Bus links from Edinburgh and from railway at nearby Tweedbank*
Parking	*Pay-and-display parking opposite the abbey (TD6 9LA)*
Toilets	*Between the abbey and Market Square*

The three Eildon Hills, with their Iron Age forts and Roman signal station, dominate a large part of Borders Region with their distinctive pointy shapes. So this tough climb of Eildon Hill North (or climbs, if you add in Mid Hill) is well rewarded. Melrose itself is worth lingering in, with handsome stone buildings, a ruined abbey, and two small gardens managed by the National Trust for Scotland. But do book into a B&B rather than sleeping out under the Rhymer's Tree…

Melrose High Street

SHORT WALKS SCOTTISH BORDERS

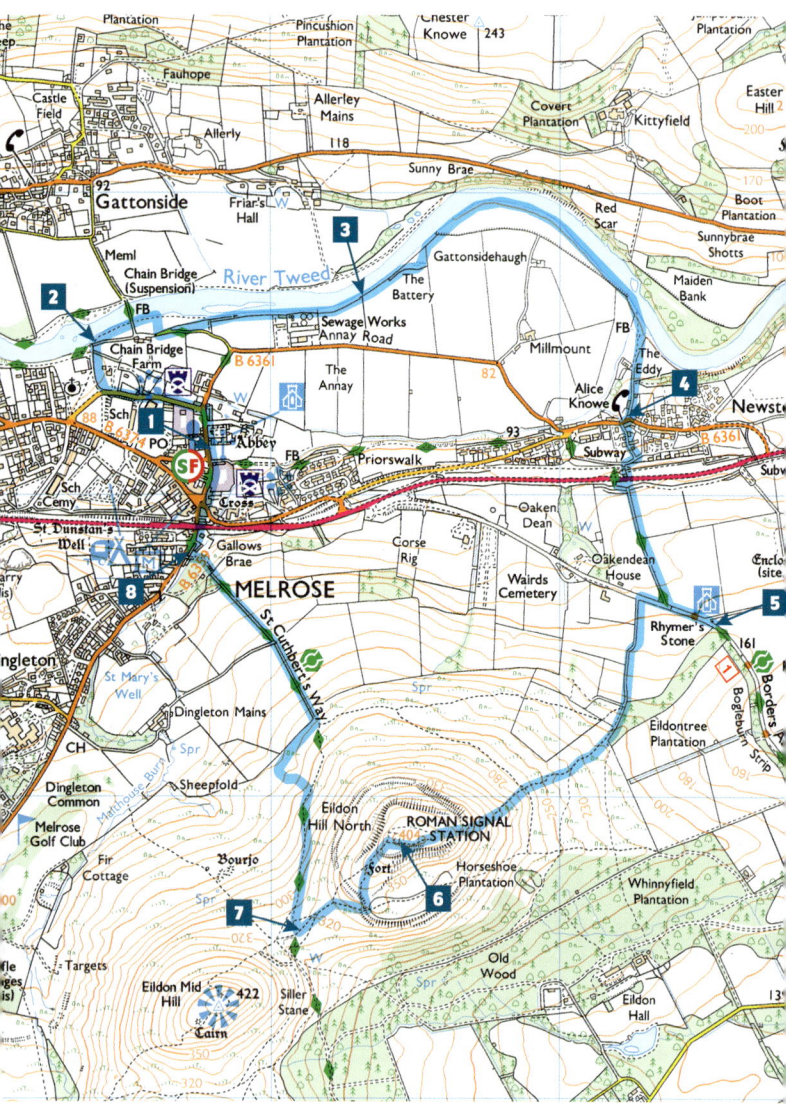

WALK 10 – EILDON HILLS

1 From the abbey, head north along Abbey Street past Harmony Gardens, bending left into St Mary's Road to pass behind the rugby pitch. Turn right onto a tarmac path to the **River Tweed**.

2 Just ahead is a stile onto an earth path to the right along the riverbank and under the **Chain Bridge**. In another 100m turn off right along a path to a tarmac lane. Turn left and at once fork left through a gate. At the field end, wiggle left then right onto a clear path. The river is on the left, not in sight at first.

3 Soon the path emerges in riverside fields. After 1km it crosses a raised boardwalk, then bends away from the river to the end of a lane into **Newstead**.

Having once provided local services to the nearby Roman camp, Newstead claims to be the oldest continuously inhabited village in Britain. The fine stonework was largely built by masons who lived here while raising Melrose Abbey.

4 Cross to the right into Claymires Lane. At its top turn right then left to

Melrose Abbey

pass under the A6091 town bypass. Up at the roadside, turn left through 180 degrees on a track. This bends uphill between hedges to an abandoned two-lane road complete with white line. Turn up left, through a barrier blocking car access, to visit the **Rhymer's Stone**.

> Thomas the Rhymer fell asleep under the hawthorn tree here and was charmed away by the Queen of the Fairies to live inside Eildon Hill for seven years. He emerged with the gift of poetry.

5 Return past the top of the hedged track you arrived on and a small parking pull-in to take a hedged pathway uphill. The path heads up steepening slopes with some stone steps to the flat summit of **Eildon Hill North**.

A Roman signal station was sited here, though nothing of it is visible today.

6 From the cairn, the obvious path towards Eildon Mid Hill becomes steep and eroded below. So head slightly to the right (northwest, towards Melrose Abbey), on a path which immediately slants down left, then turns back to the right to the wide saddle between the two Eildons. Keep right on the main path to meet the wide path of **St Cuthbert's Way**.

7 Turn back sharp right. The wide path slants north down the flank of Eildon Hill North, then turns downhill to the top of fields. The path has moved from the line shown on some OS maps. Turn right along the field tops for 250m, then down left on a

Reaching the top of Eildon Hill North

WALK 10 – EILDON HILLS

Eildon West and Eildon Mid Hill seen from the saddle

hedged path. A long, long set of wooden steps leads down to the edge of **Melrose**.

> ⓘ *The heart of King Robert the Bruce, who died in 1329, is buried at Melrose Abbey.*

8 Turn down right, under the town bypass. Cross the Market Square with its unicorn-on-a-stick cross. High Street is on your left, but keep ahead down a narrow street to return to the abbey.

– To shorten

For a shorter start and a walk of 6.5km with 330m of climb (3hr), take the tarmac path called Prior's Walk to the right of the abbey. Follow 'W' markers of Borders Abbeys Way, briefly along a back street then on a small path to Newstead (Waypoint 4).

+ To lengthen

From Waypoint 7 you can head up Eildon Mid Hill ahead: the right-hand path is the better of the two, but is still steep, loose, and stony. This adds 1km and 100m climb (about 30min).

Abbotsford House seen from its garden

WALK 11
Abbotsford and Cauldshiels Loch

Time 4hr
Distance 9.6km (6.0 miles)
Climb 220m

A long but otherwise straightforward walk by the Tweed and two lochs, around Sir Walter Scott's magnificent mansion

Start/finish	Visitor entrance to Abbotsford House on B6360 near Melrose
Locate	///patching.sunflower.signature
Cafes/pubs	Cafe at Abbotsford visitor centre (summer season only)
Transport	Train to Tweedbank station (1.5km from start), or bus to Galafoot Bridge and steps down to River Tweed upstream of Waypoint 2
Parking	Car park at start (TD6 9BQ)
Toilets	At Abbotsford visitor centre (summer season only)

Sir Walter Scott's mansion Abbotsford, with its outstanding collection of armour and weapons, is well worth visiting when open during the summer season. This walk (which can be done year-round) goes through its grounds and along the big river, then leads up through fields and woods to two small lochs. Both are rich in birdlife, while Cauldshiels is the one with the great picnic places.

River Tweed at Abbotsford

SHORT WALKS SCOTTISH BORDERS

1 Head down the track towards the **River Tweed**, passing the ticket office for Abbotsford on your left. Just before the river, take a path left under trees and fork right to join a wider path. Fork right again on a smaller path to follow the grassy riverbank for 800m to meet a path.

2 Join this wider path and enter woods alongside the river. After 600m the path bends back sharp left. After 150m look out for a small path (way-marked) turning up right, to the **B6360** road. Cross to a small path opposite, slanting up right to a kissing gate into an open field.

3 Head straight up the field to **Abbotslea Plantation**. Glenmayne house, a Baronial mansion of 1866, is seen across the river. Turn right along the foot of the wood then up beside its edge to a green track at the field top. Follow this to the right into woods. The track joins a wider one to pass above **Faldonside Loch** and reach a tarmac lane.

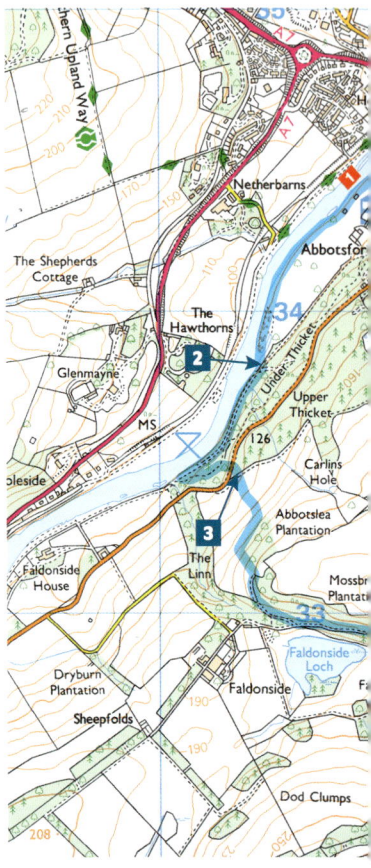

Abbotslea Plantation above River Tweed

WALK 11 – ABBOTSFORD AND CAULDSHIELS LOCH

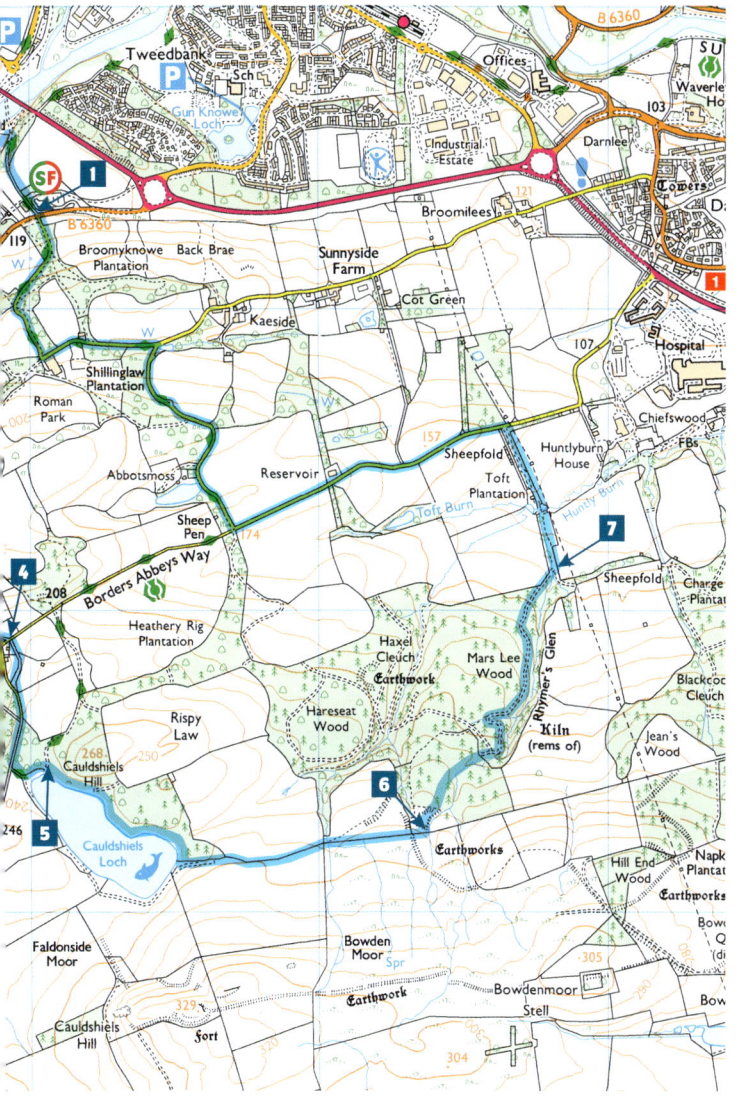

69

Cauldshiels Loch and Cauldshiels Hill

4 Cross the lane into the track opposite and follow it uphill into woods. Ignore a track forking left, but then take a path to left alongside an open field to the scrubby woods around **Cauldshiels Loch**. Turn left around the foot of the loch, to meet a wider path. The path along the south side of the loch is also usable but rough and often wet.

5 Turn right, along the lochside, to a gate into an open field below **Cauldshiels Hill**. From here there's an

Scott's collection of armour and trophies at Abbotsford

option to climb to this great viewpoint. Turn left along the foot of a large field, with scrubby wood below to start with. A path continues ahead along a fenced-in strip. With a stream ahead, the path turns left through a gate.

6 Head down through scrubby woodland. The path dodges left and back right around a side hollow, then runs down alongside the stream's little valley, the **Rhymer's Glen**, to meet a gravel track.

The Rhymer's Glen, now very overgrown, was the haunt of poet Thomas the Rhymer – the one who was seduced by the Queen of the Fairies and led into the depths of Eildon Hill (see Walk 10).

7 Follow the track left for 500m to a minor road. Turn left for 1km. At a T-junction take the side road downhill (signed as Borders Abbeys Way). Turn left at another T-junction, winding down to the walk start.

– To shorten
At Waypoint 5 turn left away from Cauldshiels Loch. The path becomes a track down to the minor road. Turn right for 600m to rejoin the main route at the T-junction. This shortens the walk to 7km with 150m climb (about 2hr 45min).

+ To lengthen
From the field below Cauldshiels Hill, head uphill to the left of a wall. Just beyond the wall top, two gates on the right give access to the hilltop fort. Up and down adds 1.5km and 100m climb (about 45min).

Williestruther Loch

WALK 12
Hawick and Vertish Hill

Start/finish	Drumlanrig's Tower, Hawick
Locate	///rave.films.patrol
Cafes/pubs	Several cafes in Hawick High Street
Transport	Fast buses from Carlisle/Edinburgh, town bus to 'Vertish Hill' stop at Waypoint 3
Parking	Car park at Upper Common Haugh (TD9 0BH), across River Teviot from walk start
Toilets	At Upper Common Haugh

Time 3¼hr
Distance 8.6km (5.3 miles)
Climb 200m

A longish walk, with a little care required with route-finding, taking in a handsome mill town with its two rivers and a small hill

Hawick has a proud history as one of the strongpoints during Scotland's War of Independence and the Border Reiving times of the 16th century; and this walk starts by exploring the traces that remain from that time. In the centuries that followed, Hawick became a centre of the weaving and woollen trades, with mills exploiting the water power of the River Teviot. After passing through the town, the walk looks down on it, first from its ancient motte and then from the small Vertish Hill.

Drumlanrig's Tower museum and visitor centre

WALK 12 – HAWICK AND VERTISH HILL

1 Pass through an arch to left of the museum entrance and turn right behind the building. Incorporated within the visitor centre block, Drumlanrig's Tower, a defensive pele tower, is the town's oldest surviving building. Cross into a short road paved with stone setts towards the steps up to St Mary's Kirk. Don't go up these steps but bear left around the base of the church mound to cross the old stone Kirkwynd Bridge over Slitrig Water.

2 Turn right along Slitrig Crescent for 300m to a fenced-in tarmac path on the right. This leads to Slitrig Water and a footbridge. The path zigzags uphill into Moat Park; head right to

The Motte in Moat Park

steps up the **Motte** mound. The mound is the rallying point for Hawick's annual riding of the town boundaries. Go back down the steps and cross grass up leftwards to the park's top corner. Turn briefly right, then left up a two-lane street called The Loan. This rises to the edge of town and dips to a mini-roundabout.

St Mary's Kirk

Track above Flex Farm

3 Turn left and bear right on a track up beside the **golf course**. Keep ahead through a gate and in another 150m look out for a less-used path forking off left. The path contours to a gate into open fields. Follow the top edge of the field to its corner under a clump of pine trees. Turn right through a gate onto a farm track, which leads with grand views down through **Flex Farm** to a minor road.

4 Turn right for 1km gently uphill, to a junction with a side road on the right. Keep ahead to visit **Williestruther Loch**. Just across its dam there's a tempting picnic table. Then return to the junction to take the side road. After 800m, having passed **St Leonards** on your right, the road bends left. Here take a signposted path back sharp right. Keep the wall on your right for a few steps, then fork left through scrub to the golf course edge.

> ⓘ *Hawick's motto 'teribus an teriodin' was its soldiers' war cry at the Battle of Flodden (1514). Nobody knows what it means or even what language it's in.*

Ospreys occasionally fish Williestruther Loch, but herons and waterfowl are commoner sightings. A pair of mute swans usually nests here; in 2024 they successfully raised seven cygnets.

5 You will be following the crest of **Vertish Hill** along the top of the golf course, northeast, with some waymark

posts. Turn right around the edge of the course to a grass track along the left edge of a strip of trees. After 100m the track joins a gravel one along the strip's right edge. Cross a fairway, with a green on your right, to a green path along the left edge of the next strip of trees. At the end of this, bend right to join a well-made path; but where this path bends down right, turn off left at a waymark post.

6 Follow the right edge of a strip of pine trees (a golf fairway on your right) to its end: there's a non-functioning drinking fountain here. Bear left to head down the left edge of trees to a teeing-off area. Pass to the right of this to find the start of a clear path behind it. This leads down to rejoin the outward route. Head downhill to the mini-roundabout.

7 Turn right to return into **Hawick**. Keep ahead down through Drumlanrig Square and Howegate back to the walk start.

> **− To shorten**
>
> On leaving Moat Park, turn down right back to the walk start; then explore along High Street as far as The Horse statue – 2.5km with 50m climb (about 1hr).
>
> **+ To lengthen**
>
> A well-built path runs right around Williestruther Loch, adding 1.5km (30min).

The Upper Lake and Bowhill House

WALK 13
Bowhill House

Start/finish	*Courtyard entrance to Bowhill House near Selkirk*
Locate	*///rush.destroyer.quaking*
Cafes/pubs	*Cafe at Bowhill House*
Transport	*No public transport*
Parking	*Main car park just above walk start (TD7 5ET, closed October to Easter), or General's Bridge car park (same postcode) just after leaving A708*
Toilets	*In courtyard at Bowhill House*

Time 3hr
Distance 7.7km (4.8 miles)
Climb 150m

Two lakes, Yarrow Water, and ruined Newark Castle, all in the grounds of handsome Bowhill House

The Duke of Buccleuch, the UK's biggest landowner by area, made it big during the cattle-thieving 16th century; his ancestor Walter Scott, the 'Bold Buccleuch', is celebrated in a border ballad for his daring raid on Carlisle Castle to rescue a henchman. When times became more peaceful, the family built the more comfortable Bowhill House, leaving the fortified Newark Castle passed on the fairly strenuous full version of the walk. The gentler short version circles the ornamental lakes, which were laid out following suggestions from family member and novelist Sir Walter Scott.

Lady's Walk by Yarrow Water

Yarrow Water, below the Lady's Walk

1 From the courtyard gateway cross the driveway and take the path up left to the main car park. There's a footpath information board here. From the top corner of the car park, don't join the track on the right but instead bear left on a footpath with a green arrow. This drops into woods and bends right. After 400m it runs alongside a woodland track. After a long footbridge, turn down to the left. Soon open ground is on the left, with views back to the house. The path crosses a track to a boathouse at the corner of **Lower Lake**.

2 Green arrows bear left (a shortcut) but turn right in front of the boathouse for the path anticlockwise around Lower Lake. Fork right at Old Pepper's Trail and take the next path left, with a black arrow, to pass around the end of the lake. Then bear right on a wide path gently uphill and after 200m join a small tarmac track.

3 After just 75m, opposite a green-and-black waymark post pointing forward, bear right on a faint path over grass and across a track. Keep ahead as it joins a wider path at two large, dead beech trees. Continue around the **Upper Lake**, anticlockwise, soon with a view across it to the house. Keep close to the lake to round its northwest corner and reach a lakeside bench. The shorter version of the walk now continues ahead.

4 At the bench, with a garden hedge seen just above, turn back sharp right on a wide path. After a gardener's cottage on your left, turn left on a wide track. Cross the main driveway of **Bowhill House** and at once turn right, with a red waymark, on a path through woods to meet another track.

5 Cross to a path (the Lady's Walk, red waymark arrows) under a strip of tall lime trees. This turns left in woods

WALK 13 – BOWHILL HOUSE

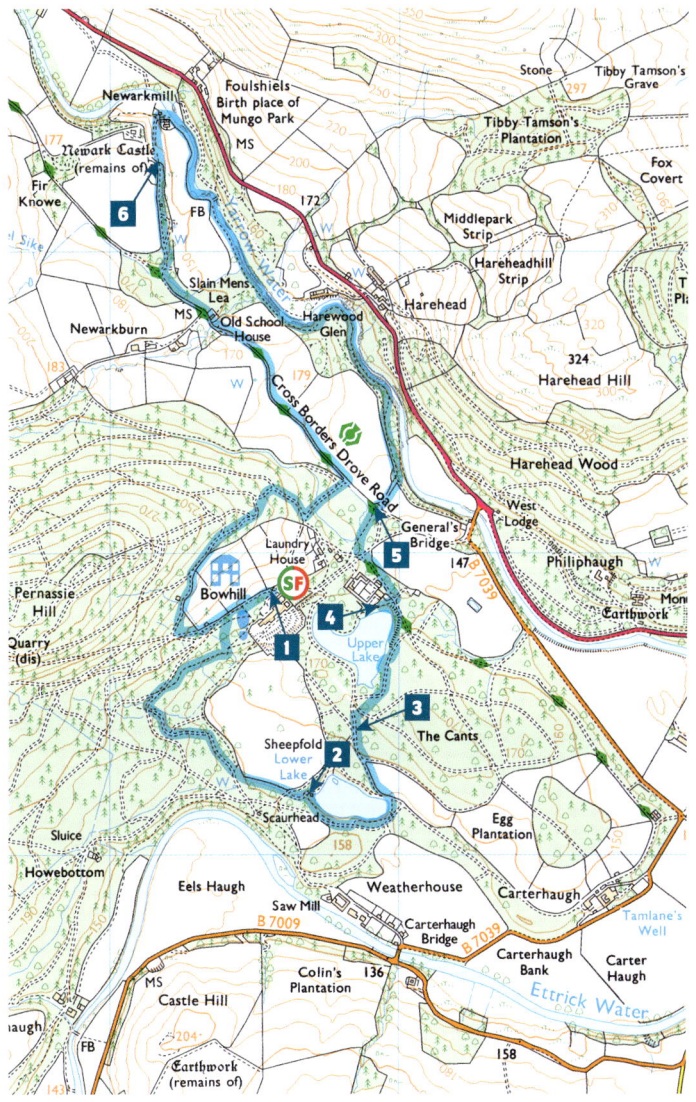

Newark Castle

> ⓘ *Pele towers are border strongholds designed for protection during the Reiving Times of the 15th century – cows on the ground floor, people overhead.*

above **Yarrow Water**. In 200m fork right, down to the riverside. After 2km the riverside path reaches **Newarkmill**. Turn away from the river up the driveway to where it meets a tarmac estate road.

Seen just up to the right, the old tower house Newark Castle was the scene of a horrible massacre of 100 civilians by Scots 'Covenanters' supporting Oliver Cromwell. The name means 'New Work', or new construction, which it was in 1423.

Looking across to Newark Castle and Foulshiels Hill

WALK 13 – BOWHILL HOUSE

6 Turn left along the estate road. In 1.2km, where woods start on the right (and 150m short of Waypoint 5), turn right up an unsigned woodland track. In 200m, with open ground ahead, take the track up right, with a yellow arrow. Keep left at junctions, also with yellow arrows. The track runs along the top of an open field looking down on the main car park, then descends to a track junction. Turn left to the main car park above **Bowhill House**.

– To shorten
From Waypoint 4 keep ahead along the lake shore, until a small tarmac track runs up right to the main driveway close to Bowhill House. This reduces the walk to 3.5km with 50m climb (about 1hr 30min).

+ To lengthen
For wider views of the surrounding country, at Waypoint 6 turn up right to pass Newark Castle. Where the tarmac track bends right, turn sharp left on a hedged track, with views back over the castle before it drops to rejoin the main route. Adds 0.8km (about 15min).

Tweed Bridge and parish church, Peebles

WALK 14
Peebles and Neidpath Castle

Start/finish	South end of Tweed Bridge, Peebles
Locate	///ruins.pizzeria.strides
Cafes/pubs	Cafe at Eastgate Theatre, pubs and cafes in Peebles High Street
Transport	Frequent, fast buses from nearby towns and Edinburgh
Parking	Car park at Kingsmeadow, below walk start (EH45 9EW)
Toilets	At Kingsmeadow

Time 2hr
Distance 5.9km (3.7 miles)
Climb 50m

A town, a tower, a riverside – and a tunnel. A torch will be useful on this one

After exploring a couple of ancient churchyards, this walk takes you on a fairly rough path alongside the River Tweed and under the impressive border strongpoint of Neidpath Castle. After a railway viaduct high above the river, the return route is through a 700m-long railway tunnel – a torch is advised, though a phone will just about do. For those who prefer to stay above ground, the riverside alternative has even better views of the castle.

Tweed riverside walk above Peebles

Mercat Cross in Peebles

1 Downstream from the road bridge you'll see a white suspension footbridge. Head down steps to the riverside and walk along the riverbank (toilets and large car park on your right) to cross the footbridge. Turn briefly left, then right along the edge of open ground. Pass round to the right of a church (the gate and steps ahead being closed), up Tweed Brae to the High Street. Peebles High Street has many fine old buildings; the Mercat Cross, mid-street, features a wind vane and vertical sundials.

2 Cross to the Eastgate Theatre (a former church, with a cafe round to the right). Turn left past the Mercat Cross, then right into Northgate. Immediately turn left down Bridgegate and cross the Tree Bridge over Eddleston Water, then continue up Bridgegate to a junction.

Bridgegate, locally 'Briggat', is the former drove road for herds of cattle, which passed through the town and then over the Manor Hills towards the markets of England.

3 Keep ahead up Old Church Road to Cross Road. Turn left to pass the gate to the ruined **Cross Kirk**. Keep on along Cross Road and its continuation St Andrew's Road to the graveyard of St Andrews Kirk, with an entrance just to your right. Pass notable graves beside the tarmac path to the church

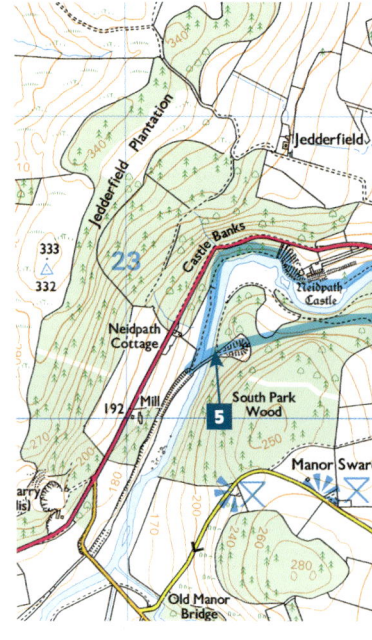

Cross Kirk ruins

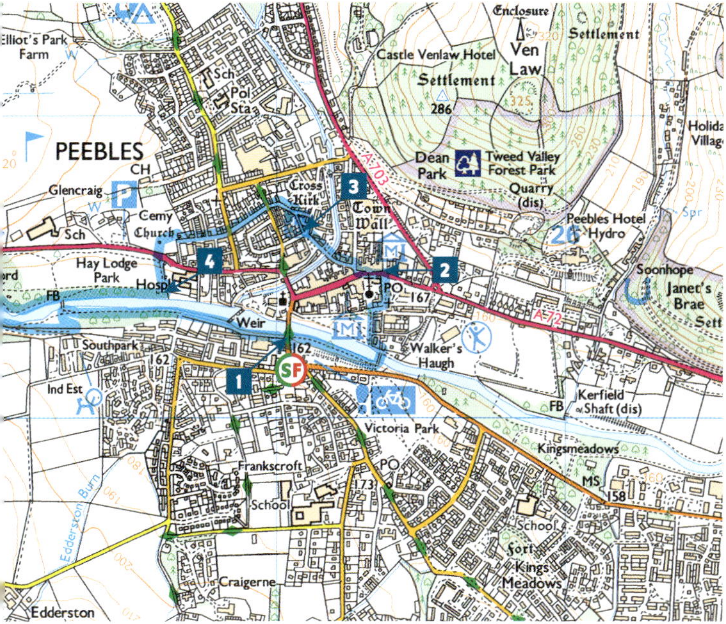

SHORT WALKS SCOTTISH BORDERS

tower. One grave features an early 18th-century couple, him in his kilt and high heels. Turn left and exit to the main A72. Cross into **Hay Lodge Park**, heading down to the riverside.

4 Turn upstream alongside the river. At the end of the park, bear left on a rugged path along the riverside. This passes below **Neidpath Castle** to the former railway viaduct. Head to the right up steps, to cross the viaduct.

5 Ahead, the railway path dives into a long, dark tunnel. Alternatively, at the viaduct end turn left for the rough riverbank path. At the tunnel end, continue for 400m, then take a path down sharp left to a white footbridge over the river. Don't cross but turn downstream along the riverside until a ramp leads up onto the Tweed Bridge.

> ⓘ *Peebles's crest is three salmon, with the motto 'incrementum contranando' – I increase by swimming against the flow.*

Neidpath Castle and the Tweed

— To shorten

From the north (town centre) end of Tweed Bridge, turn left down a ramp past the swimming pool to head upstream beside the river, missing out the loop through the town. Gives a walk of 4.5km (1hr 30min).

Neidpath Castle

Neidpath Castle, now used as a wedding venue, is a classic Borders tower house and served to defend against cattle raiders from neighbouring glens as much as against the English army. Built in the 1390s, it was attacked with cannons and captured by Oliver Cromwell's forces in 1650. Mary Queen of Scots and Sir Walter Scott slept at the castle; and William Wordsworth wrote a poem condemning the felling of 'a brotherhood of ancient trees' growing around it.

Leaving Cademuir West hill fort

WALK 15
Cademuir Hill

Start/finish	*Manor Sware viewpoint above Peebles*
Locate	*///wildfires.straws.indulges*
Cafes/pubs	*Wide choice in Peebles*
Transport	*No public transport*
Parking	*Small car park at Manor Sware (EH45 9JE) – approach from Peebles as the road from the west is closed to traffic*
Toilets	*No public toilets on route*

Grassy Cademuir has great views and two Iron Age forts – both of which have visible stonework remains, while the western one also has defensive *chevaux-de-frise*, which are spiky stones to deter horse riders. The return walk is on a path alongside the Tweed. Some hill paths are faint and there's one steep but short descent after the western fort.

Time 3¾hr
Distance 8.8km (5.5 miles)
Climb 250m

A small, grassy hill, two impressive hill forts, and a return along the broad River Tweed

Beside River Tweed, upstream from Old Manor Brig

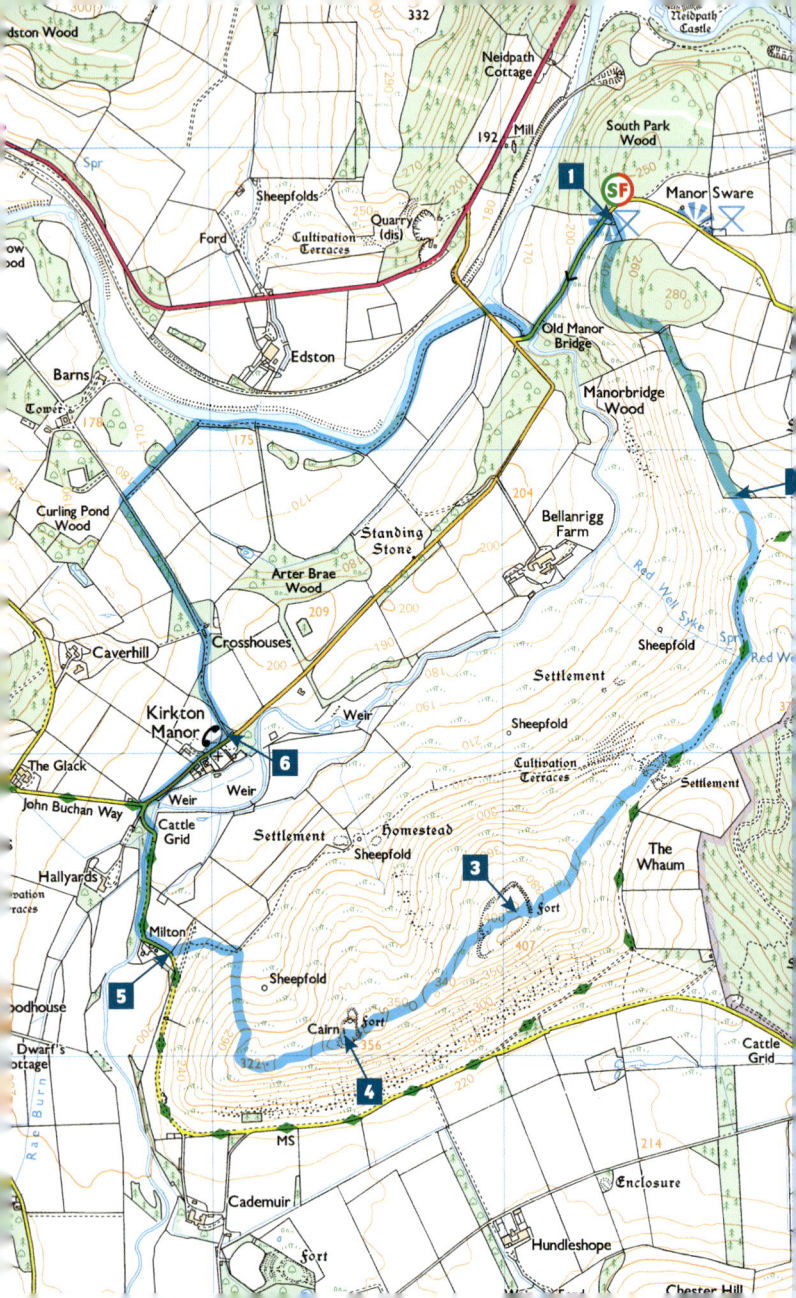

Path onto Cademuir Hill

1 A path runs uphill from the parking area into a wood. At once turn right on a wide path running above the foot of the wood. In 400m fork right on a smaller path, which drops through a wall gap, and head up inside a narrow wood strip to a ladder stile over a wall. Note that some dogs may have difficulty with this high stile.

2 A grass path leads uphill to join the wider path of the **John Buchan Way** (a 'book' emblem is on its waymarks). Turn right, past a waymark post. The wide path slants gradually up the flank of the hill onto its main ridgeline. Follow the path as it runs along the ridge, passing through settlement remains. At the start of the next rise, the John Buchan Way bears down left, but instead keep ahead up to the 407m summit **fort** with its earth and stone rampart. Cademuir's name is from Gaelic *Cadh Mor*, meaning the great battle – but nobody knows who fought whom, or who won.

3 Follow the undulating ridgeline down ahead (south of west), with steep drops and great views on the left. A faint path runs slightly down to right of the crest at first. The ridgeline levels off to a dip with *chevaux-de-frise* stones before the western Cademuir **fort**.

SHORT WALKS SCOTTISH BORDERS

4 Exit steeply down through the former west gateway to the ridge tip, where there's a small satellite dish (community broadband). In front of this turn to the right along a faint path down to the top end of a field wall. Here turn down left, on a path slanting away to the left of the wall to reach the small road at **Milton**.

5 Turn right to Manor Water, where you pass picnic tables, then cross a bridge with ornamental trellis railings. Follow the main road to the right towards **Kirkton Manor**. Pass a church on your right to reach a driveway track on the left with a small lodge and concrete gateposts.

6 Turn up the driveway for 800m, then watch out for a stile and gate on the right, waymarked 'Tweed Walk'. A grass track leads down to the **River Tweed** and bends right, downstream. Continue down the riverside path and pass under a stone-arched road

Chevaux-de-frise on Cademuir Hill

bridge. The path bends right, with Manor Water to its left, to a small road closed to traffic. Turn left over **Old Manor Bridge** or Brig and back up to Manor Sware.

> **— To shorten**
> At Waypoint 6 continue along the quiet road to Old Manor Bridge for a walk of 8.5km with 150m climb (about 3hr 15min).

View of Tweed valley from Manor Sware

USEFUL INFORMATION

Tourism bodies

Scotland Tourism
www.visitscotland.com

Historic Environment Scotland
www.historicenvironment.scot

National Trust for Scotland
www.nts.org.uk

Tourist information centres

VisitScotland has closed or is closing local tourist information centres in favour of information provided online.

Berwick-upon-Tweed
tel 01670 622155
www.visitberwick.com

Travel

UK Journey Planner
www.traveline.info

Trains
www.scotrail.co.uk

Further reading

The Steel Bonnets: the story of the Anglo-Scottish Border Reivers, George Macdonald Fraser (1971)

Minstrelsey of the Scottish Borders, Walter Scott (1803) – border ballads collected (and improved) by the author

Battle Valleys: a portrait of the Border, Ronald Turnbull (2012)

The Marches: border walks with my father, Rory Stewart (2016)

© Ronald Turnbull 2025
First edition 2025
ISBN: 978 1 78631 251 8
eISBN: 978 1 78765 170 8

Printed in Singapore by KHL Printing on responsibly sourced paper.
A catalogue record for this book is available from the British Library.
All photographs are by the author unless otherwise stated.
Cover illustration of Neidpath Castle by Avery Mitchell.

© Crown copyright and database rights 2025 OS AC0000810376

Cicerone's EU representative for GPSR compliance is Easy Access System Europe, Mustamäe tee 50, 10621 Tallinn, Estonia. Email gpsr.requests@easproject.com.

CICERONE

Cicerone Press, Juniper House, Murley Moss, Oxenholme Road,
Kendal, Cumbria, LA9 7RL

www.cicerone.co.uk

Updates to this Guide

While every effort is made to ensure the accuracy of guidebooks as they go to print, changes can occur during the lifetime of an edition. Any updates that we know of for this guide will be on the Cicerone website (www.cicerone.co.uk/1251/updates), so please check before planning your trip. We also advise that you check information about transport, accommodation and shops locally. Even rights of way can be altered over time. We are always grateful for information about any discrepancies between a guidebook and the facts on the ground, sent by email to updates@cicerone.co.uk.

Register your book: To sign up to receive free updates, special offers and GPX files where available, create a Cicerone account and register your purchase via the 'My Account' tab at www.cicerone.co.uk.